JORDAN MARIE BRINGS THREE WHITE HORSES WHETSTONE

Also by Andrew Maraniss

For Children:

Beyond the Game: Maya Moore

Beyond the Game: LeBron James

Beyond the Game: Pat Tillman

For Teens:

Strong Inside (Young Readers Edition): The True Story of How Perry Wallace Broke College Basketball's Color Line

Games of Deception: The True Story of the First U.S. Olympic Basketball Team at the 1936 Olympics in Hitler's Germany

Singled Out: The True Story of Glenn Burke

Inaugural Ballers: The True Story of the First US Women's Olympic Basketball Team

For Adults:

Strong Inside: Perry Wallace and the Collision of Race and Sports in the South

Beyond the Game
ATHLETES CHANGE THE WORLD

JORDAN MARIE BRINGS THREE WHITE HORSES WHETSTONE

by Andrew Maraniss
Illustrated by DeAndra Hodge

VIKING

VIKING

An imprint of Penguin Random House LLC
1745 Broadway, New York, NY 10019
penguinrandomhouse.com

Text copyright © 2025 by Andrew Maraniss
Illustrations copyright © 2025 by DeAndra Hodge

Penguin Random House values and supports copyright. Copyright fuels creativity, encourages diverse voices, promotes free speech, and creates a vibrant culture. Thank you for buying an authorized edition of this book and for complying with copyright laws by not reproducing, scanning, or distributing any part of it in any form without permission. You are supporting writers and allowing Penguin Random House to continue to publish books for every reader. Please note that no part of this book may be used or reproduced in any manner for the purpose of training artificial intelligence technologies or systems.

Viking & colophon are registered trademarks of Penguin Random House LLC.

Edited by Kelsey Murphy
Design by Anabeth Bostrup
Text set in Baskerville Regular

Library of Congress Cataloging-in-Publication Data is available.

First published in the United States of America by Viking, an imprint of Penguin Random House LLC, 2025

Manufactured in the United States of America

LSCC

ISBN 9780593526248 (hardcover)
1st Printing

ISBN 9780593526255 (paperback)
1st Printing

The authorized representative in the EU for product safety and compliance is Penguin Random House Ireland, Morrison Chambers, 32 Nassau Street, Dublin D02 YH68, Ireland, https://eu-contact.penguin.ie.

For Alison, Eliza, and Charlie —A. M.

To the Missing and Murdered, you are never forgotten. —D. H.

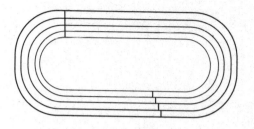

BEYOND THE GAME

A Note about the Series

"A life is not important except in the impact
it has on other lives."
—Jackie Robinson

BEYOND THE GAME tells the stories of remarkable athletes to convey lessons on empathy, justice, and social good. As a parent of elementary school–aged kids, I worry about the profound problems we are leaving for our children to solve. Even concepts as basic as truth and democracy are in peril.

We tend to admire athletes for their strength, speed, and victories. But this series does not celebrate athletes solely for their athletic feats. Instead, it chronicles those who have used their platforms to help other people. Not merely by writing a check, posing for a photo, or showing up in the community for a day, but through extraordinary acts of courage and selflessness.

Of course, this doesn't mean the subjects of these books are perfect. Athletes are human, after all.

But in a way, that's the point.

The people featured in this series are inspiring, not because athletes are more important or better than anyone else, but because in revealing their humanity they challenge the rest of us to act, too.

"Any time you have an opportunity to make a difference in this world and you don't, then you are wasting your time on this earth."
—Roberto Clemente

BEYOND THE GAME:
ATHLETES CHANGE THE WORLD

JORDAN MARIE BRINGS THREE WHITE HORSES WHETSTONE

CHAPTER ONE

MITAKUYE OYASIN.

As a child growing up on the Lower Brule Sioux (Kul Wicasa Oyate) Reservation in South Dakota, Jordan Marie Brings Three White Horses Whetstone (previous family name Daniel) heard these words often.

Mitakuye oyasin: "We are all related."

For Jordan's family and other members of the

Lakota Nation, the idea that everything is connected holds special meaning about love and community. It means caring not only for all people as equals but animals and nature, too. Humans, pets, prairies, mountains, and streams were all placed on this planet by the Creator for a reason. All have a spirit and are worthy of respect.

The Lakota people have lived in this balanced and empathetic way for thousands of years. Before colonization, the Tribe lived on lands that stretched from present-day South Dakota, Nebraska, and Wyoming, north to Montana and east to Minnesota.

When European settlers arrived on the shores of North America in the fifteenth century, between seven and ten million Indigenous people from more than five hundred Tribes lived in what is now the United States and Canada—from the Iroquois in the Northeast to the Choctaw in the South, from the Hopi in the Southwest to the Inuit of the Arctic. But as these European colonizers began to claim Native land as their own, they expanded their settlements westward by displacing Indigenous peoples from their ancestral homelands through violence, deception, and theft.

Despite the terrible damage inflicted by centuries of colonialism, including war, disease, and broken treaties, the Lakota culture and belief system survived. Families passed down traditions and culture from generation to generation, including to Jordan's mother, Terra Beth. Only eighteen years old when she gave birth to Jordan in 1988, Terra Beth worked hard to put herself through college and nursing school while raising her baby girl. And when Jordan was still an infant, her mom started dating the man Jordan has always considered her father, a white graduate student, psychologist, and comedian named David Daniel.

Jordan grew up surrounded by her extended family in rural South Dakota, including her grandparents and cousins. She was taught to respect her elders, and she considered her young mom her best friend. Jordan loved to play outside with her cousins on the green rolling hills of her hometown, even though she was the kind of kid who tripped and fell a lot. She loved canoeing in the Missouri River, swimming in the summer, and sledding in the winter. When she wasn't outside, she enjoyed playing with toy cars, watching Disney movies, and reading picture books about Native American history, learning the traditions of different Tribes and the stories of heroic figures such as Olympians Jim Thorpe and Billy Mills.

Most of all, Jordan loved spending time with her lala, her grandfather, Nyal Brings Three White Horses.

Nyal's life was a combination of tragedy and triumph. Born in 1937, he grew up on the Rosebud Reservation in South Dakota in a house with no electricity or running water. When he was nine, he was taken from his parents and placed in a reservation boarding school. Like many of these notorious

schools designed to strip Native children of their culture, Nyal's school was an abusive place where white teachers forced him to give up his Lakota language and traditions.

But Nyal persevered. He was the first person in his family to graduate from college. He dedicated his life to helping other Indigenous people, becoming a Tribal health director and a youth sports coach.

As a young man, Nyal had been a star athlete. Running gave him a sense of freedom and a chance to shine. He starred in middle-distance events, earning All-American honors at the University of South Dakota. In two races, he beat a future Olympic gold medalist and fellow Native American from South Dakota named Billy Mills. Nyal had hopes of competing in the 1960 Summer Olympics. But he was badly injured in a car crash and had to give up his dream.

He then passed his passion for running on to his daughter, Terra Beth. She became one of the fastest sprinters in her age group and was training to compete at the 1988 Olympic Trials when she found out she was pregnant with Jordan. Like her father, she too had to give up her Olympic dream.

But the family tradition continued. Jordan inherited a love of running from her mom and grandfather. A fast runner in playground games as a kid, she would go on to win state titles in high school and compete at the highest level in college.

And one day, as an adult, she would combine her

love for running and for her people with a burning desire to fight injustice. She would use her platform as an athlete to advocate for vulnerable people and a ravaged planet. Yet Jordan Marie Brings Three White Horses Whetstone's greatest victory wouldn't come by being the first to cross a finish line.

It would come by making the world a better place.

CHAPTER TWO

IN HER CHILDHOOD summers, Jordan often spent more time with her father, David, than her mother. While Terra Beth studied to become a nurse, David was putting himself through graduate school with a job that required a lot of travel. He wasn't a truck driver, soldier, or salesperson—he was a stand-up comedian.

That meant he spent long hours driving across

the country from one comedy club to another, earning money for the family by making people laugh. When Jordan was off from school in the summer, she traveled with her dad, giving her mom more time to study.

Jordan loved the long drives with her dad. They'd sing along with songs on the radio, pump their arms to dare truck drivers to honk their horns, and always stay at hotels with a pool. She would unpack her clothes and toys and carry blankets and pillows into the closet so she could sleep in her own cool and dark cave. By the time she was nine years old, she'd been to every state except Alaska and Hawaii.

One day, her parents told her that the family

was moving across the country so her father could take a job as a professor in Maine. Jordan was excited. But she was thinking more about the fun drive to Maine than about actually living there and leaving her family and friends behind.

At first, everything new and different about living in the small town of Farmington, Maine, was exciting for nine-year-old Jordan. She had never been surrounded by so many tall trees and mountains. She had never lived in a two-story house. Her bedroom had a window seat, where she could sit and read and gaze outside.

Yet soon the trees seemed to close in on her and the small town didn't seem so friendly. Nobody else at her school looked like her. For the first time in

her life, Jordan noticed that other people treated her differently because she had brown skin.

She didn't feel connected.

She felt alone.

CHAPTER THREE

JORDAN'S FAMILY HAD moved from South Dakota because there were more jobs and opportunities for them in Maine. That may have been true, but for Jordan, the move came at a cost.

Every day at school, she was reminded she didn't fit in. Not only was she the "new kid" and the only Indigenous student, but she was also the only one who wasn't white. Some kids made ignorant, racist comments about her heritage, like "I didn't know Indians still existed," and "I thought you were all extinct."

Jordan felt embarrassed. Worse, she felt ashamed to be Native American. She didn't want to be reminded she was different all the time. She wished she didn't have brown skin. She felt completely disconnected from her culture.

Some of her classmates' parents wouldn't let Jordan come to their houses to play or allow their kids to visit Jordan's home. They'd say that Jordan was a bad kid or a bad influence and that she was probably going to steal something. These comments were based on false, bigoted stereotypes.

Once, in eighth grade, Jordan and her friend Jeff

were walking home from school when a group of older kids came up and started calling Jordan terrible names. The bullies pulled out knives and brass knuckles. They pushed Jeff and yelled at him for "hanging out with an Indian."

Jordan ran as fast as she could to her father's office at the university.

She was safe. But she was shaken. This wasn't the kind of running she liked.

Running was something that usually brought Jordan joy, something that connected her to her family in South Dakota. Her love for running began when she was ten years old. Her family had gone back to South Dakota for a summer vacation. One day her grandfather Nyal took her out for her first long run, one mile downhill to start and one mile back up the hill to finish.

At first, Jordan hated it. *How could anyone think this is fun?* But she enjoyed spending time with her lala, who always encouraged her. She liked being outside in nature, and she liked the way her body moved and her mind relaxed. She was fast and strong.

Back in Maine, running became the one part of Jordan's life that connected her to the people around her. She made friends with the other kids at school who enjoyed running. On her middle school and high school track and cross-country teams, nobody teased her or made her feel less than equal. Instead, people cheered for her. Terra Beth took on the role of team mom, hosting sleepovers, painting signs to hold up during races, and screaming at the top of her lungs at the track meets.

As Jordan advanced through middle school and high school, her mom gave her advice, kept her stats, and tracked her splits (the time it takes to run a specific distance) in the middle of competitions. She didn't put pressure on Jordan, but it was obvious she was pushing her to set goals and focus on achieving them.

Jordan's dad took a different approach. Rather than obsess about Jordan's times, David half-jokingly told her to "run stupid" and to not overthink things. To stay calm, stay present, and just do her thing.

The combination of influences worked wonders, and Jordan emerged as one of the top runners in the

state. Her performances drew the attention of college coaches, and she eventually earned an athletic scholarship to the University of Maine.

Things seemed to be going her way.

Beneath the surface, however, Jordan was suffering.

CHAPTER FOUR

GOING BACK TO her junior year of high school, Jordan had stopped eating enough food.

At first, she ate only healthy foods to get in better shape and run faster times. But soon, she hardly ate any food at all. She wrongly believed that not eating was a way to take control over her life when she felt anxious, sad, or upset. She would eat a bite of chicken or some vegetables in front of other people just for show. But mainly she ate trail mix. And that was it. Jordan lost way too much weight. Her body lacked the nutrients it needed.

One day in her second year on the team in college, Jordan could barely finish a routine run. She was pale and her legs felt as heavy as cement blocks. Her coach could tell there was something seriously wrong. He told her to see a doctor for tests.

The results were shocking: her body was low in iron, potassium, and every other important nutrient. Jordan's coach told her to forget about competing and focus on her health. He helped her create a nutrition plan, and he helped her understand that food was not the enemy. Food was fuel.

Around the same time, Jordan got some more good advice from one of her Native American professors. He could tell that Jordan was suffering in another way. She needed the nourishment not just of food, but of community. While the Lower Brule was two thousand miles away in South Dakota, there were other Indigenous families nearby. He suggested Jordan attend an upcoming round dance at the Penobscot Reservation.

She took his advice, and from the moment she arrived at the ceremony, everything felt like home: the smell of the fry bread, the beat of the drums, the laughter of the women who reminded her of her grandmothers.

Mitakuye oyasin.

Jordan felt the connection and purpose she'd been missing. The effect was profound. She was proud to be an Indigenous woman. No longer would she feel ashamed to be who she was.

As Jordan continued her studies in college, she believed she was finally in a healthy place, both mentally and physically.

And she began to thrive.

As a junior and senior on the track team, she set University of Maine records in the 3,000 meters, the mile, and the distance medley relay. She also rose to the number two position on the cross-country team. Wherever she competed, people knew her name. But more importantly, Jordan knew more about herself and what mattered to her. She remembered a goal she'd set in eighth grade. Someday, she had promised herself, she'd work in Washington, DC, to help promote Native American causes.

It was time to follow that dream.

CHAPTER FIVE

AFTER GRADUATING FROM college and moving to Washington, DC, Jordan continued to take her running seriously. She even began to make money as a runner, earning a sponsorship from a shoe company.

Jordan ran in 10Ks, half-marathons, and marathons for her sponsor's team. Even when she wasn't competing, Jordan still ran. Rather than drive or take the subway to work, she ran six miles through the city streets and monuments to and from her office every day.

DC is one of the most important cities in the world. The White House, the US Capitol building, the monuments, the world's embassies, the museums—it all adds up to a city buzzing with action.

But it's a long way from the halls of power in DC to the people in Indian Country who Jordan wanted to help. She did the best she could. Working for the National Indian Health Board, she helped Indigenous people share their experiences and opinions with lawmakers. Working for the US Department of Health and Human Services, she helped Tribes secure funds to preserve their languages and culture, support small businesses, and provide educational programs for kids.

She even took an internship with a congressional representative from Maine and launched a blog called *Native in DC*, sharing her observations on how the federal government operated.

But the more she persisted, the more disappointed she became. She had wanted to work in the nation's capital because she knew her people had been treated unjustly for hundreds of years. But in DC, she felt powerless to make real change. When lawmakers made decisions, they rarely considered the impact on Indigenous people. And powerful people still believed outrageous stereotypes about Native Americans. One man told her he thought they still lived in tepees.

Jordan was frustrated. But she wasn't going to give up. So, she looked for other ways to stand up for justice. She protested the name of DC's NFL football team, which was a terrible slur against Indigenous people. She volunteered for an organization that helped Native American people living in poverty. She even began to teach herself the Lakota language, a vital piece of her family's identity that had been stripped away years ago when her grandfather was beaten for speaking it at the Native American boarding school.

Even after all she accomplished, Jordan still saw herself more as a follower than a leader. She would hold up signs at events other people organized. She would stand and listen as other people spoke. She was much more comfortable behind the scenes than behind a podium.

But all that was about to change.

A group of courageous Indigenous teens were running two thousand miles, from North Dakota to DC, and they needed her help.

CHAPTER SIX

IN THE SPRING of 2016, young Indigenous people in North Dakota began to speak out against a project that threatened to destroy sacred cultural sites and the clean water supply at the Standing Rock (Sioux) Reservation. A Texas company planned to build an oil pipeline directly beneath a reservoir that provided the Tribe's drinking water. Many of this company's other pipelines had spilled or leaked toxins into the environment. If this were to happen in North Dakota, the Tribe's drinking water—and the water of people living downstream—would likely be poisoned.

To raise awareness for their cause, these Native American teenagers planned a relay run all the way from North Dakota to DC, a two-thousand-mile trek to collect signatures opposing the pipeline and generate publicity.

Jordan was a runner. The kids were coming to her town. She strongly believed in their cause. She knew she had to help.

So, for the first time, Jordan stepped out from the shadows and took the lead on a project. It was her responsibility to ensure the runners had no problems once they arrived in DC. She arranged for permits and a police escort. She raised money for food and water. She made sure the youth were able to speak to the media about the purpose of their run and to deliver 140,000 signatures of protest to the United States Army Corps of Engineers.

The day the runners arrived was filled with singing, drumming, prayer, and powerful testimony. The students stood up for the environment and for the rights of their Tribe against the greed and inhumanity of the oil company. And Jordan's hard work helped it all run smoothly. But she was exhausted. The stress of organizing such an important event, and the long hours it took to get all the work done, had worn her out.

"It was really great and inspiring," she later

said, "but I never wanted to do it again!"

And then Jordan received shocking news. Her grandfather Nyal had passed away.

The last thing Jordan had spoken to her lala about was the work she was doing to organize the Indigenous teens' relay events in DC. He had been so proud of her. Now Jordan felt crushed. Her grandfather was her superhero. He had inspired her to run and to speak up for her people. He meant everything to her.

Jordan returned to South Dakota for her grandfather's funeral and to spend time with her family. But it felt empty without him around. She had no interest in running. What was the point?

Soon, the answer became obvious.

In Standing Rock, protests against the oil pipeline had grown. This was a heroic example of ordinary people fighting a powerful business and a traumatic reminder of the injustices directed at Native Americans in the past.

It was also a conflict that was dripping with environmental racism, a case where a community of color was unjustly affected by an action with harmful consequences for public health. And it highlighted the differences in how Native Americans and many others in our society view their relationship with the natural world around us. Was the environment to be respected and protected, or was it a resource to extract and profit from?

The people of Standing Rock made it clear what

they believed: clean water over profits, humanity over corporate greed. They held signs that said MNI WICONI—WATER IS LIFE. But their pleas did not stop the oil company. Instead, the company brought in huge bulldozers to cut a two-mile path through an area that contained Indigenous graves and other sacred artifacts. It brought in guard dogs from Ohio to intimidate the protestors. It hired a private security firm led by former soldiers who treated the people protecting their land, water, and ancestors' graves like an opposing army.

When Jordan saw footage of the guard dogs biting some of the same kids she had met in DC, she knew she had to do more. No longer could she feel sorry for herself because her grandfather had died.

Acting on behalf of her people was the best way to channel her grief and honor his memory.

She asked herself, "If these young people are willing to stand up against these big machines, dogs, Mace, and guns, what am I doing with my life?" She began to think about running in a new way, too. It didn't have to be just about winning races, staying in shape, or finding a sponsor. It could also be about standing up for causes she believed in.

Soon Jordan would have a chance to prove it. And in doing so, she would go on to educate and inspire thousands of people.

CHAPTER SEVEN

IN THE HOURS before the start of the 2019 Boston Marathon, Jordan called her mother with an unusual request: Could she bring her some red paint?

Her mom wasn't sure why Jordan wanted it, but she brought the paint. And then, as Jordan's partner, filmmaker Devin Whetstone, drove her to the race, Jordan opened the can of paint and began drawing letters on her arms and legs. They spelled out

MMIW. Next, she covered her hand in paint and pressed it over her lips and cheeks, leaving a bold red handprint over her mouth.

The letters stood for Missing and Murdered Indigenous Women. The handprint symbolized the silenced voices of those women, victims of violence throughout the hundreds of years since Christopher Columbus and his men bragged of assaulting and enslaving countless Indigenous women and girls.

Jordan knew murder was the third leading cause of death for Native women, occurring at ten times the national average. She had learned about the connections between "man camps" of non-Native oil and gas workers and violence against Native women. She understood that a lack of communication between

Tribal, state, and federal law enforcement allowed too many missing person cases to slip through the cracks. She also saw that the media was much more likely to cover the stories of missing white women than women of color.

So, as she prepared to run in one of the most prestigious marathons in the world, Jordan decided to spotlight these problems. She would honor the memories of women society had forgotten.

As Jordan ran through the streets of Boston, the red handprint and letters drew the attention of spectators and photographers. And at the start of each mile of the 26.2-mile race, Jordan spoke the name of a murdered or missing woman out loud and said a prayer in her memory. She had done research on all

these women and knew details of their lives and disappearances. Women such as Britney Tiger, Savanna LaFontaine-Greywind, and Victoria Jane Eagleman. Real people with real families. Stories that deserved to be told. Families who deserved to be heard. Communities that deserved respect and attention.

As she ran the last steps toward the finish line, Jordan said one final prayer, this one for her lala. In her head, she could hear him call out, "You got this, girl!" like he had so many times before.

Jordan finished the race in three hours, two minutes, and eleven seconds. She wasn't sure how many people had noticed her red paint, and she assumed only other Indigenous people would understand its significance. And that would have been enough.

So, it came as a shock when she discovered her advocacy had gone viral. Photos of Jordan running in red paint had been shared tens of thousands of times on social media. Her Instagram account grew from three thousand to fifty thousand followers in one day. Podcast hosts and reporters from sports and news magazines and websites wanted to talk to her about her advocacy.

Suddenly, people across the country knew Jordan's name, and more important, they learned about an issue they might not have known about otherwise. Jordan had proven that sports activism can make a difference. A few days later, she received a message on Instagram with the best news yet.

Jordan had inspired another young athlete to take action.

CHAPTER EIGHT

GROWING UP IN the state of Washington as a member of the Cowlitz Tribe, Rosalie Fish often felt like she was the only Indigenous girl who enjoyed running. Many times, she was the only girl from her Tribal school who competed in track meets. Rosalie also played basketball. After one game, she went in the bathroom and discovered hateful, racist messages scrawled on the wall.

The slurs and the hate inspired Rosalie to compete for more than just herself. She felt that when she ran, she represented all Indigenous people.

Rosalie knew all about MMIW. She'd seen the missing person posters on her reservation and heard stories from her family. Her aunt, Alice Looney, had gone missing when Rosalie was just three years old. At first, Rosalie thought this was just a problem on her own reservation. But as she learned more, she discovered this was a problem across the US and Canada.

Rosalie felt hopeless. What could she do that would make a difference?

Then she learned about what Jordan had done at the Boston Marathon. Watching another Indigenous woman running with confidence gave Rosalie a jolt of inspiration. She found Jordan's Instagram page and sent her a direct message. She asked for permission to follow Jordan's example and wear red paint at her state track meet. Rosalie knew people would be watching her compete. How could she use the opportunity to help others?

Jordan wrote back immediately with an enthusiastic "yes!" She called Rosalie her mithankala, little sister, and encouraged her to call or text anytime for support. At the state finals, Rosalie competed in the 400-meter, 800-meter, and 2-mile runs. She painted a red handprint over her face and ran each race in honor of a different murdered or missing woman from her reservation.

She felt the stares and the judgment from people who did not understand what she was doing or didn't approve. But she knew she was running for an important cause, which inspired her to push herself like never before. She had won the 800-meter and 2-mile races. But she still had the 400-meter run left to go, and she was tired.

The 400 was not her favorite distance. But before she stepped back on the track, her coach gave her some words of encouragement. She reminded Rosalie that we are all connected. That Rosalie was running not just for herself or for the women she intended to honor, but for all the girls back at the Tribal school and for Indigenous women everywhere.

That day Rosalie ran better than she ever had in

the 400, recording a personal best time and finishing second in the state. But she was less proud of her results than of representing the women with "integrity and strength."

When Jordan found out the news, she was elated.

"Indigenous people are constantly fighting their own erasure," she said, "and it's exhausting to have to be that constant voice to speak up." It felt good to have someone else stand beside her. Jordan hoped that other Native American teens would follow Rosalie's example. And soon, they did. A girls' high school basketball team in Arizona wore jerseys with the names of murdered and missing Indigenous women on the backs. A boys' cross-country team competed with red handprints on their faces.

Connections were made. Awareness increased.

Then, in 2024, Vice President Kamala Harris hosted a reception in honor of the most important women in sports, and she invited Jordan.

The movement gained strength.

CHAPTER NINE

TODAY, JORDAN LIVES in Virginia with her husband, Devin, and their three young children. She says she has entered a new stage of her running career. She's not as concerned with winning races or setting personal bests. She gives herself grace when her times are not as fast as they once were.

But that doesn't mean running is not important to her. It's just about something different. Her trail

runs are about connecting with nature: looking at the sky, smelling the trees around her, feeling the crunch of the leaves beneath her feet. It's about remembering her lala and honoring her family. It's about representation—showing that Indigenous people will not allow themselves to be erased and aren't just found in history books. And it's about advocacy and running for something bigger than herself.

Jordan continues to fight for justice, mostly through Rising Hearts, a nonprofit organization she founded. The group raises awareness of MMIW. It calls on organizers of marathons and other footraces to acknowledge that their events are taking place on stolen Native lands. It supports families whose relatives suffered at American Indian boarding schools.

But Jordan does not limit her advocacy to Indigenous people. She says she "can't stand" to see anyone excluded or treated unfairly. And she says that in a country of many cultures, it is important to remember that we all have a purpose. She says to think of our society like a puzzle. Every person represents one piece, and all pieces are equally necessary to make the whole. No one should be treated as lesser than.

We are all related.

Mitakuye oyasin.

LEARNING FROM JORDAN

When Jordan was the new kid at school in Maine, she felt excluded by most of her classmates because she was different. When a new student joins your school, how could you make them feel welcome? How do you treat kids who are considered different in your community?

Jordan said her grandfather was her superhero and biggest inspiration. When he died, she vowed to fight for justice in his honor. Are there people in your family or town who inspire you to do good in the world? Who and why?

At first, Jordan was more comfortable supporting

causes than leading them. Why are both roles important? What does it take to be a good leader? What does it take to be a good supporter?

When you think about the Lakota idea of *mitakuye oyasin* ("we are all related"), how does it influence the way you treat the people, animals, and nature around you?

If you are an Indigenous person, which parts of Jordan's story can you relate to and why? What are the injustices you'd like to resolve in your community? If you are not Indigenous, what are the ways you can support Indigenous people in your community and in the nation?

GET INVOLVED

Jordan encourages young people to get involved in their communities and become advocates for justice.

"Whether you inspire one person or thousands," she says, "your impact on the world is needed."

If you and your family are interested in learning more about the issues discussed in this book, Jordan says you can discover a lot online. "Google and learn about issues. If you're not Indigenous, find out if there are Indigenous people in your community or a reservation nearby. Become a good ally and help them organize. Don't overstep. Help them get a platform where their voices can be heard."

RESOURCES FOR CHILDREN AND FAMILIES

IllumiNative: IllumiNative.org

National Indian Education Association: NIEA.org

National Museum of the American Indian: AmericanIndian.si.edu

Native America TV series: PBS.org/show/native-america

Project 562: Project562.com

Rising Hearts: RisingHearts.org

We R Native: WeRNative.org

WoLakota Project: WoLakotaProject.org

RESOURCES FOR ADULTS

National Indigenous Women's Resource Center: NIWRC.org

Orange Shirt Society: OrangeShirtDay.org

Sovereign Bodies Institute: Sovereign-bodies.org

Urban Indian Health Institute: UIHI.org

GLOSSARY

Advocacy: Public support for a cause or policy

Billy Mills: Oglala Lakota runner who won a gold medal in the 10,000 meters at the 1964 Olympics in Tokyo, coming from behind in a dramatic finish.

Boston Marathon: The world's oldest annual marathon, begun in 1897. Held on the third Monday of April.

Energy Transfer: Pipeline company that built the controversial Dakota Access Pipeline. Hired dogs and militarized private security to oppose citizens of Standing Rock Reservation. Headquartered in Dallas but incorporated in

Delaware, which some companies do to avoid paying certain taxes. Had $89 billion in revenue in 2022. Jersey-patch sponsor of the Texas Rangers.

Environmental racism: A form of injustice in which communities of color face a disproportionate number of environmental hazards. The Dakota Access Pipeline was originally scheduled to cross the Missouri River near the city of Bismarck, North Dakota. That plan was then changed to have it cross under the river by the Standing Rock Reservation. This was considered by many to be a prime example of environmental racism because the controversial project was moved away from a whiter, wealthier, and more politically powerful community to a less powerful community of color.

Extraction: Withdrawing materials from the environment for use by humans

Indigenous people: Native to a particular region. Often preferred over "Native American" in certain contexts.

Lakota: One of three branches of the Sioux people (Dakota and Nakota are the other two). Notable Lakota in history include Sitting Bull and Crazy Horse. Kul Wicasa Oyate refers to the band of the Lakota known in English as the Lower Brule.

Round dance: Traditional Indigenous event featuring drumming to celebrate life and bring people together. Participants form a circle, hold hands, and move slowly to the beat of the music. It's a time for fellowship, togetherness, and community.

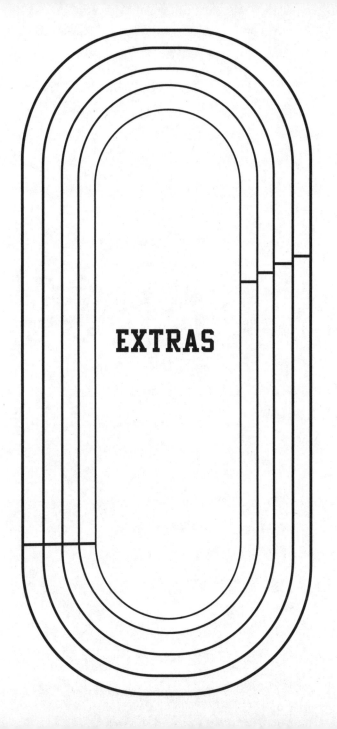
EXTRAS

LISTS

INDIGENOUS US OLYMPIC MEDAL WINNERS

Name/Tribe	Year	Site	Event	Medal
Jim Thorpe, Sac and Fox	1912	Stockholm	Pentathlon, Decathlon	Gold
Duke Kahanamoku, Native Hawaiian	1912	Stockholm	100-meter freestyle	Gold
Lewis Tewanima, Hopi	1912	Stockholm	10,000 meters	Silver
Billy Mills, Lakota	1964	Tokyo	10,000 meters	Gold

INDIGENOUS WORDS IN EVERYDAY ENGLISH

Word	Tribe
bayou	Choctaw
caribou	Algonquin
caucus	Algonquin
chipmunk	Ojibwe
moccasin	Algonquin
opossum	Powhatan
pecan	Ojibwe
raccoon	Powhatan
squash	Narragansett
toboggan	Algonquin

US STATE NAMES BASED ON NATIVE AMERICAN WORDS

LAKOTA TERMS

apetu ki le	today
ate	father
ble	lake
bloketu	summer
caje	name
canpaza	tree
hoksi	child
huku	mother
hunka	ancestor
ihá	smile
iyuski	happy
lala	grandfather
lila pilamayaye	thank you very much

maste	sunshine
mni	water
ohitika	courage
owáyama	school
oyate	the People, Tribe, or Nation
suka	dog
taskatapi	basketball
Unci Maka	Grandmother Earth
wahca	flower
wakta	hope
wi	sun
wóyute	food

MORE NOTABLE NATIVE AMERICAN ATHLETES

Name	Tribe	Sport	Achievement
Clarence Abel	Ojibwe	Hockey	Pioneering Olympian and NHL star
Notah Begay III	Navajo	Golf	Four PGA Tour victories
Charles Bender	Ojibwe	Baseball	Hall of Fame pitcher
Ellison Brown	Narragansett	Running	Two-time Boston Marathon winner
Jacoby Ellsbury	Navajo	Baseball	Two-time World Series champion
Joseph Guyon	Ojibwe	Football	Pro and College Football Hall of Famer
Madison Hammond	Navajo/Pueblo	Boxing	First Native American NWSL player
Janee' Kassanavoid	Comanche	Hammer Throw	First Native World Championships medalist

Gabby Lemieux	Shoshone	Golf	First Native American LPGA golfer
Cheri Madsen	Omaha	Wheelchair racing	Four-time Paralympian
John Meyers	Cahuilla	Baseball	Played in four World Series
Frank Pierce	Seneca	Running	First Native American Olympian (1904)
Kali Reis	Wampanoag	Boxing	World champion boxer
Lauren Schad	Lakota	Volleyball	International pro volleyball player
Louis Tewanima	Hopi	Running	Olympic silver medalist (1912)

FOR A NEW FICTION SERIES FROM ANDREW MARANISS, CHECK OUT SPORTS ZONE!

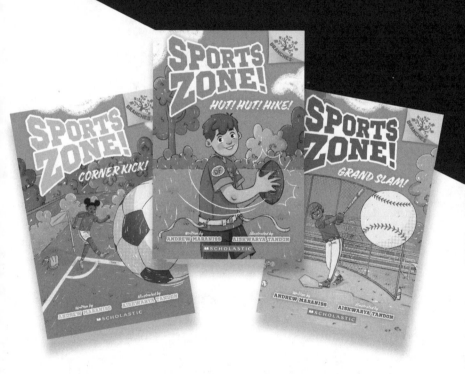

SCHOLASTIC and associated logos are trademarks and/or registered trademarks of Scholastic Inc.

READ MORE IN THE *Beyond* THE GAME SERIES!

THIS is the story of WNBA star Maya Moore. While known as one of the greatest basketball players of all time, Maya Moore has changed the world beyond sports.

AVAILABLE NOW!